Blaze of Glory

Coloring Book

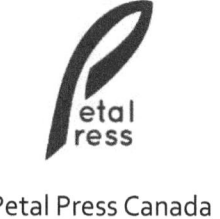

Petal Press Canada

This coloring book is licensed for your personal enjoyment only. All rights reserved, including the right to reproduce this book, or a portion thereof, in any form. This book may not be resold or uploaded for distribution to others.

Copyright © 2017 M. Garzon

ISBN: 978-1988844015

All rights reserved

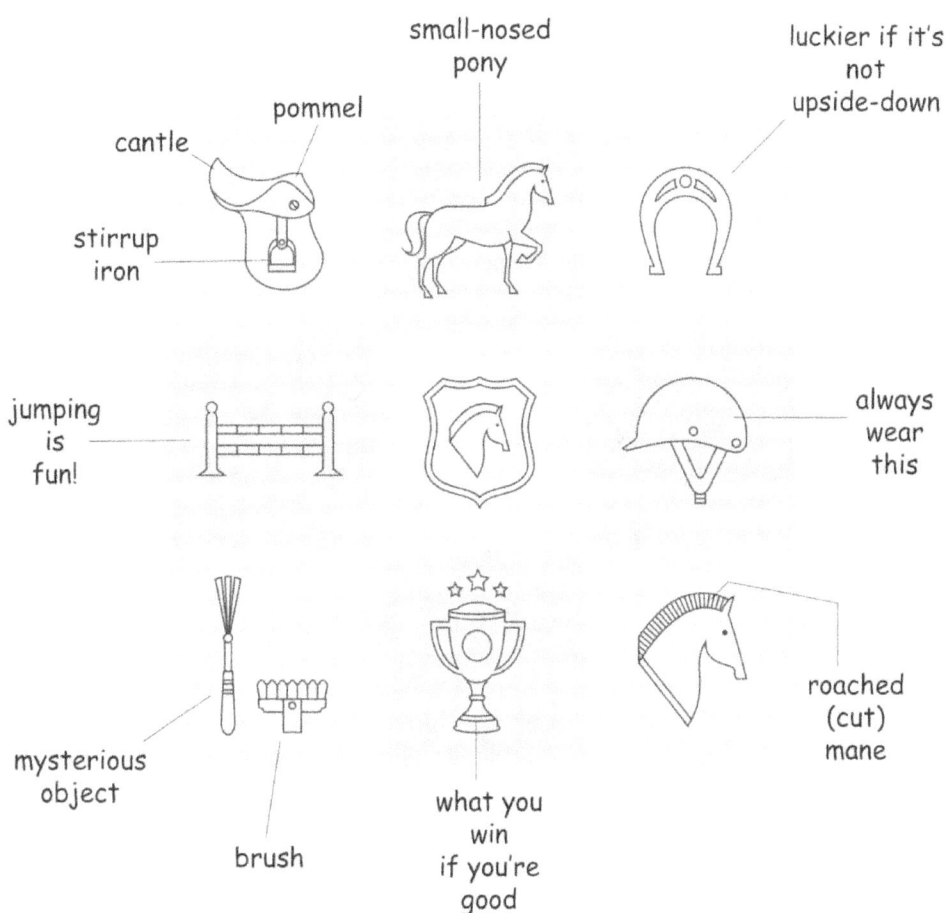

"And God took a handful of southerly wind, blew his breath over it, and created the horse." – Bedouin legend

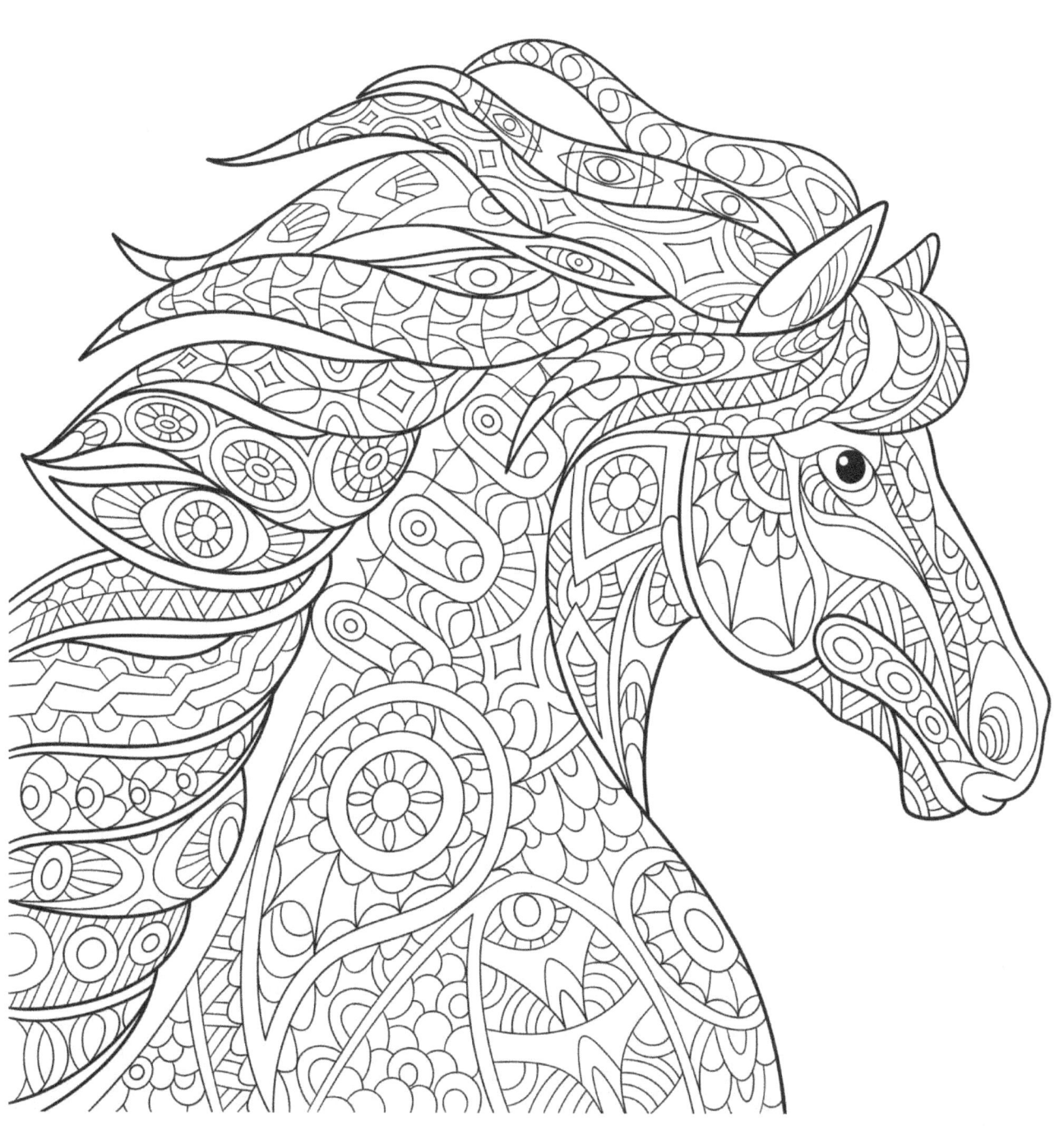

Téa

I was going to ride.

I rode almost every day, yet it still thrilled me. Not in the way it used to, when it was novelty to merely sit on a pony's back. Now, thrills arose both from the simplest of things, and the most complex.

A horse's breath, blowing on my palm.

The incomparable, indescribable smell of horse.

Moments of union so complete, my thoughts alone shape our movement.

The horse my full partner, meeting me more than halfway.

A joyful duo, dancing to silent music.

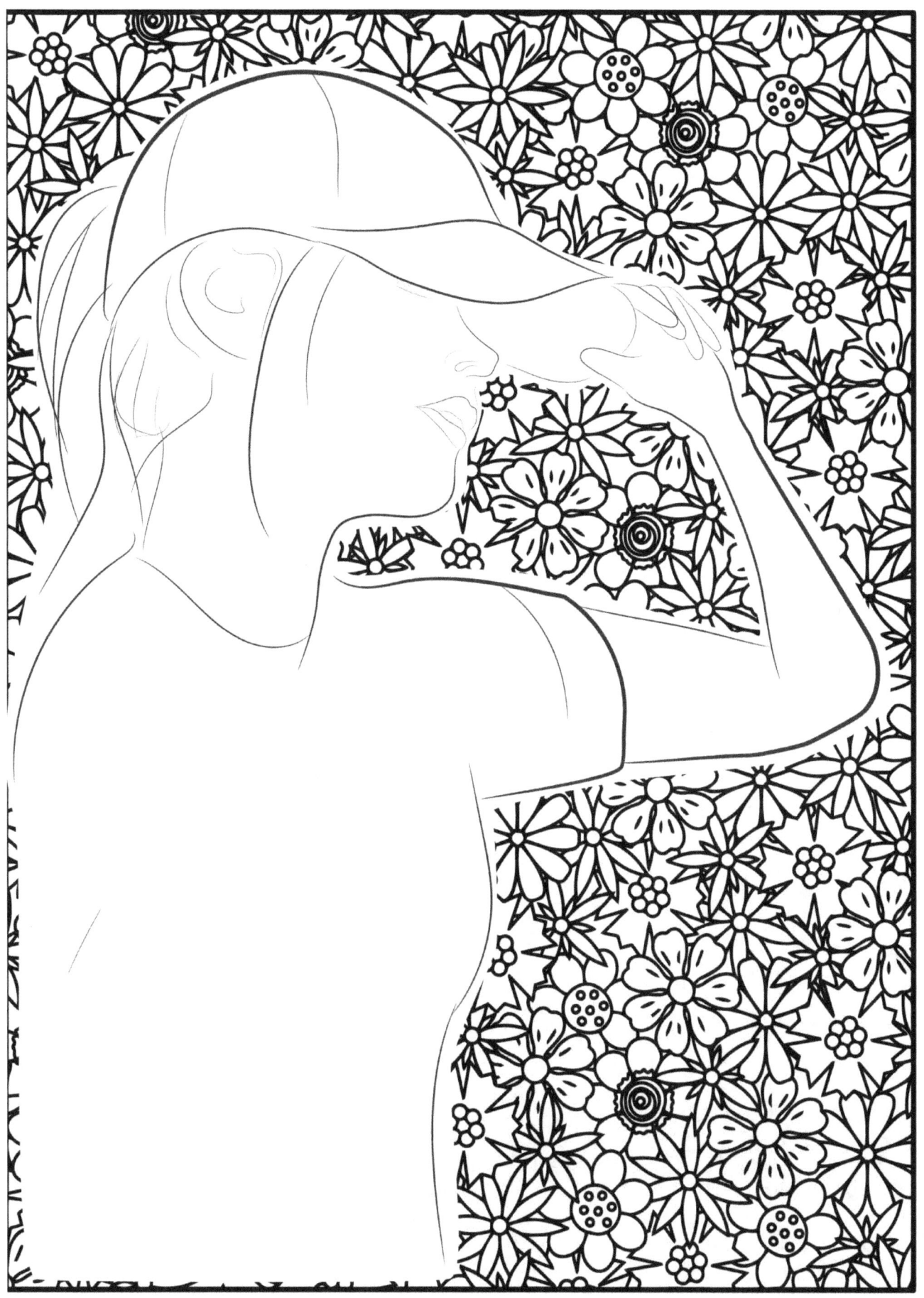

"In riding a horse we borrow freedom." – Helen Thompson

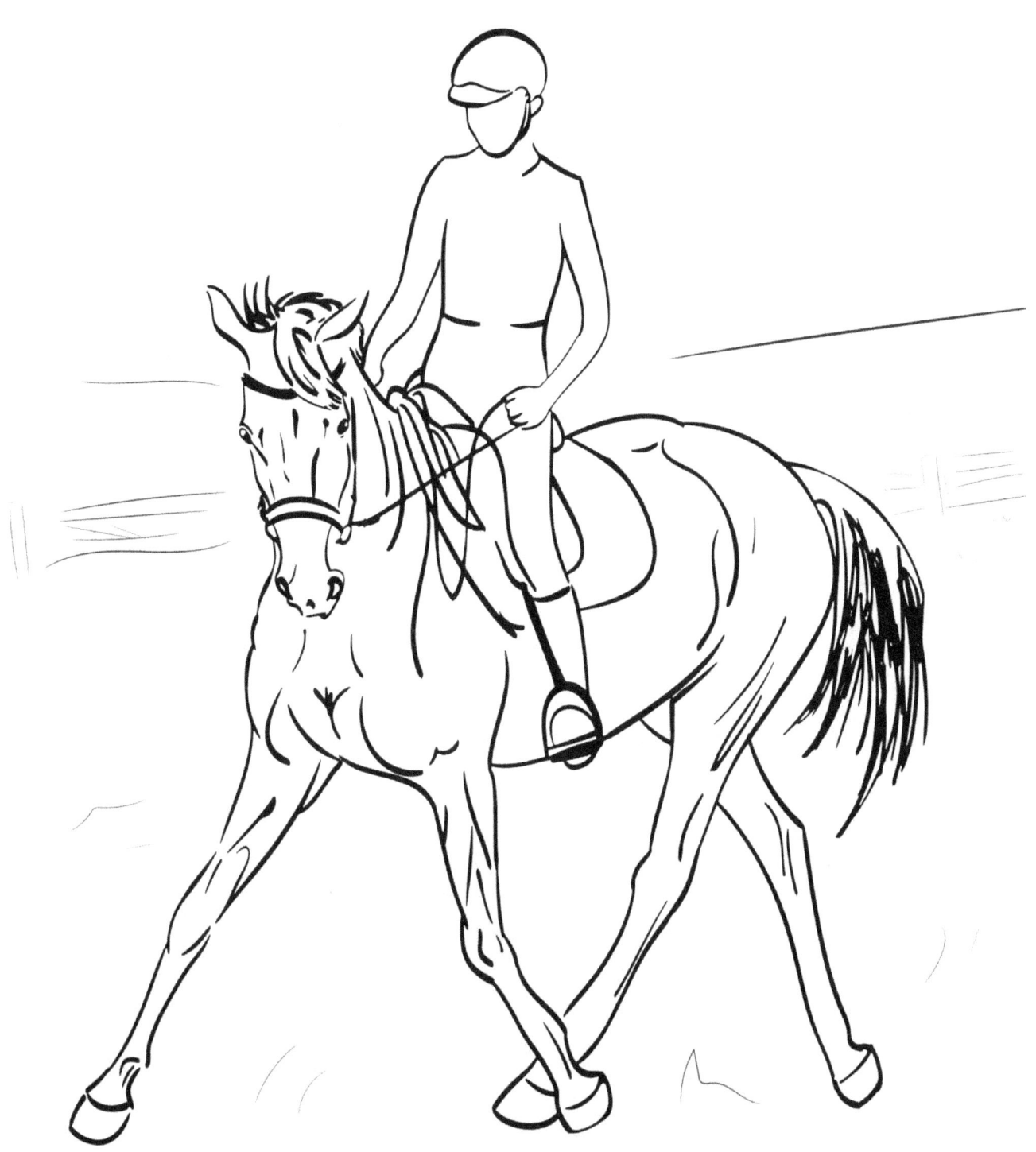

Birds aren't meant to be caged, and when they are, they're not really birds anymore.

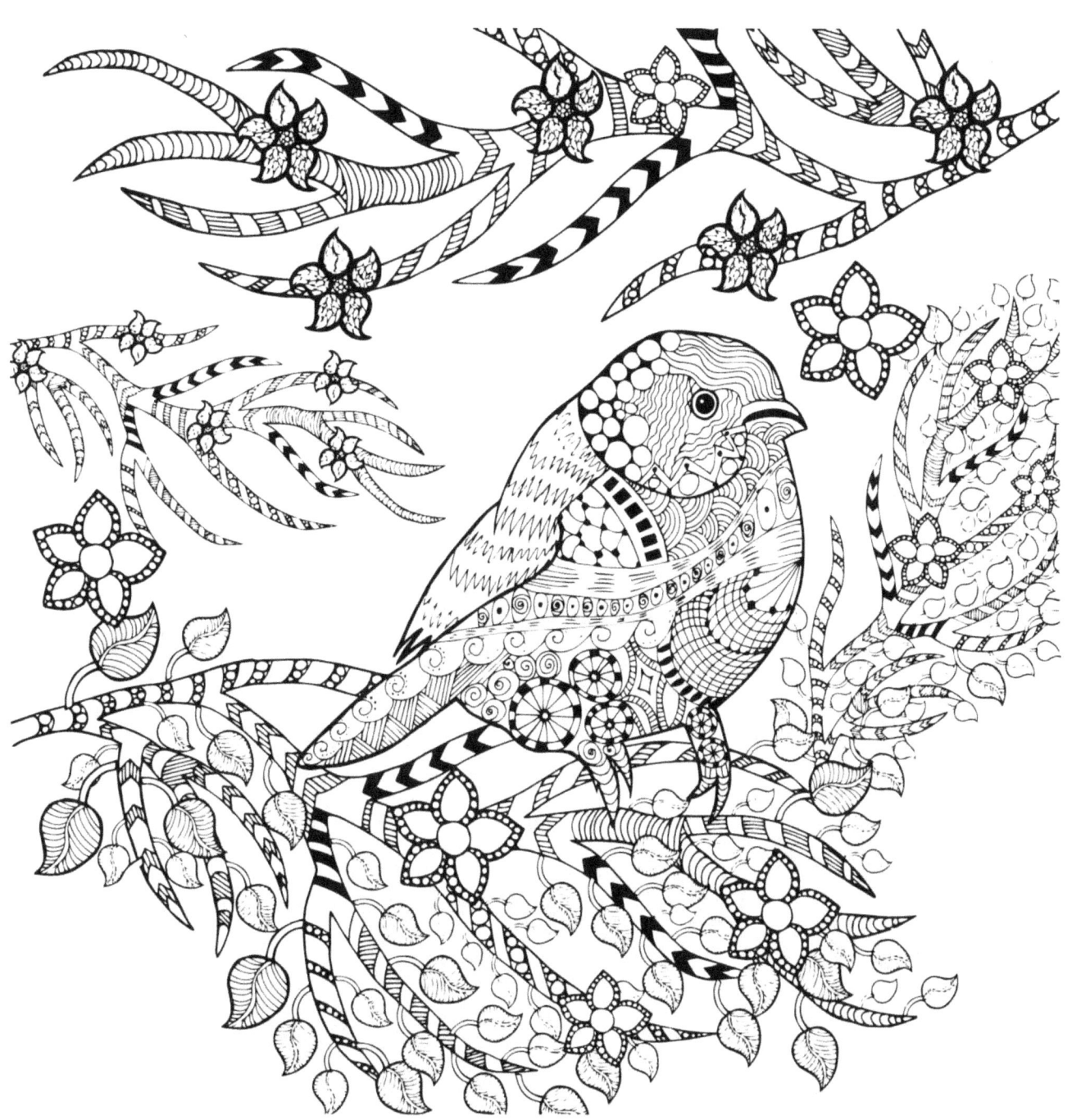

"The wind of heaven is that which blows between a horse's ears." – Arabian Proverb

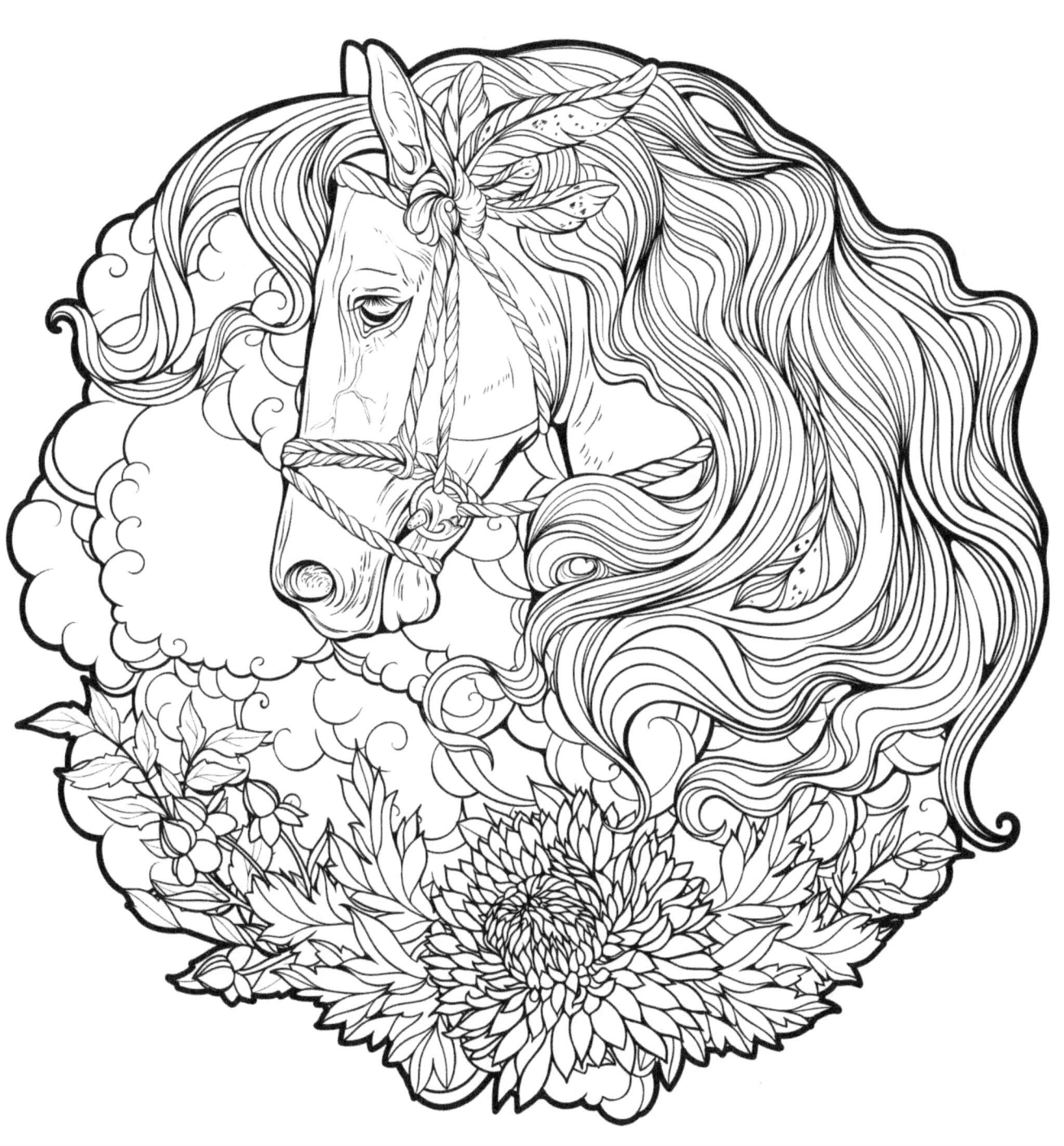

Seth

Seth was sunshine. He was grassy meadows and gentle breezes. There was nothing of darkness or sharpness in him. Sometimes, in my blackest moments, I thought he was too good for this world.

Seth's motto:

"It's hard to be a human. Play nice."

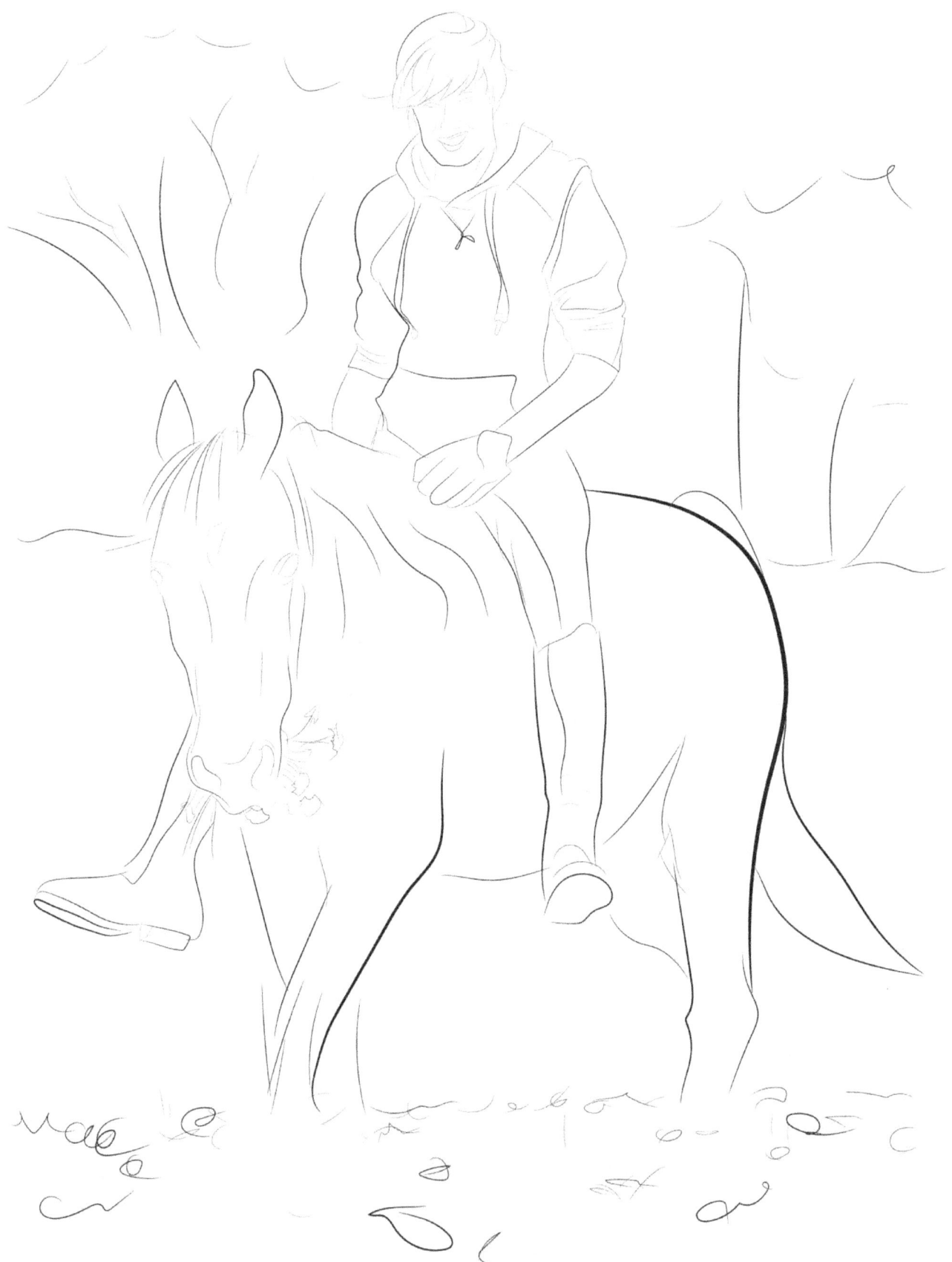

The mythical kelpie is a supernatural water horse. It has the head, neck and mane of a normal horse, legs like a horse, webbed feet, and a long, two-lobed, whale-like tail. It's said to haunt Scotland's lochs and lonely rivers.

The kelpie appears to victims as a lost, dark grey or white pony that can be identified by its constantly dripping mane. It entices people to ride on its back before taking them down to a watery grave.

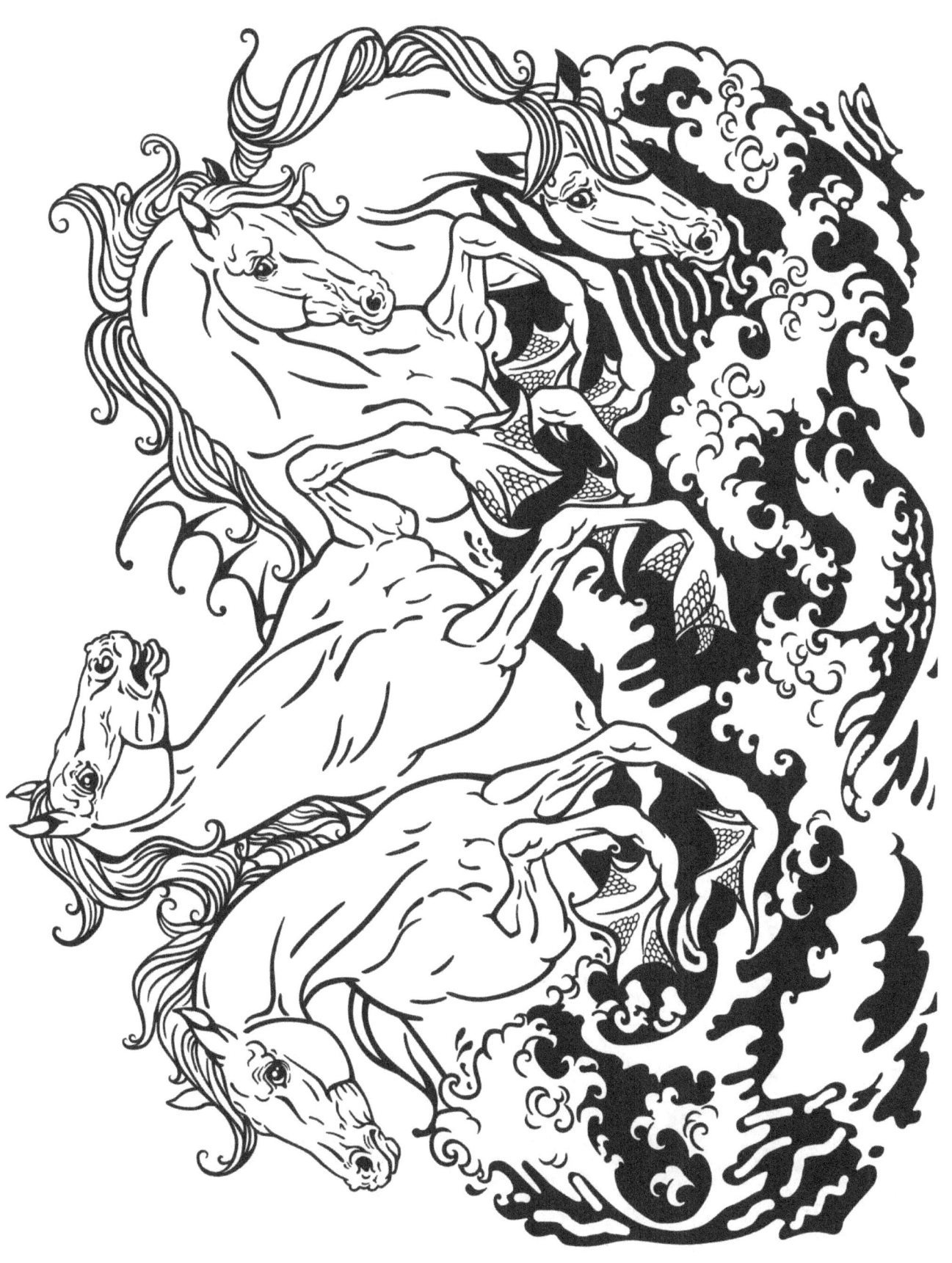

Love is a leaf unfolding,

Love is a dog's soft ear,

Love is the sky exploding,

Love is always near.

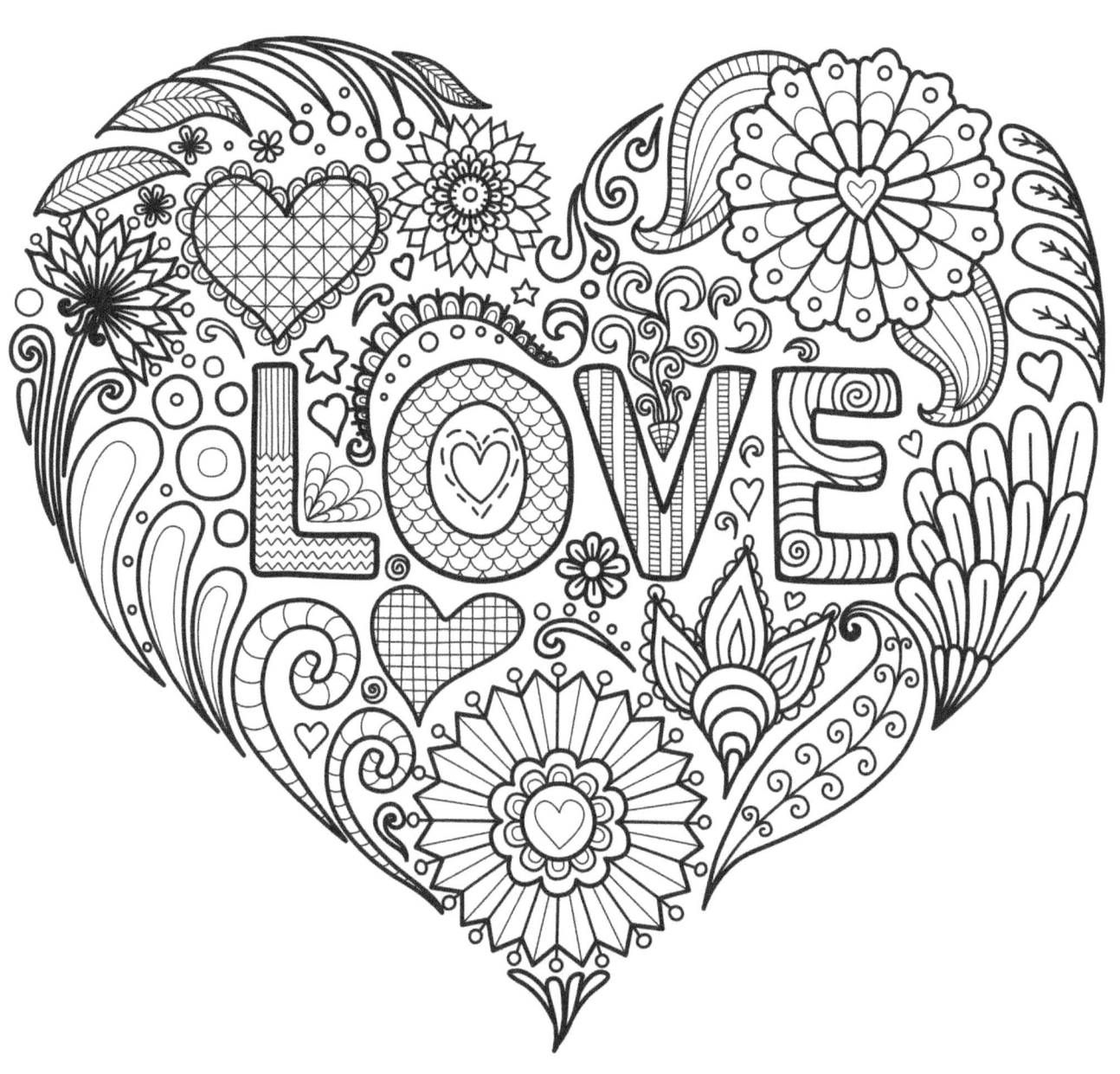

"Horse sense is the thing a horse has which keeps it from betting on people."

– W.C. Fields

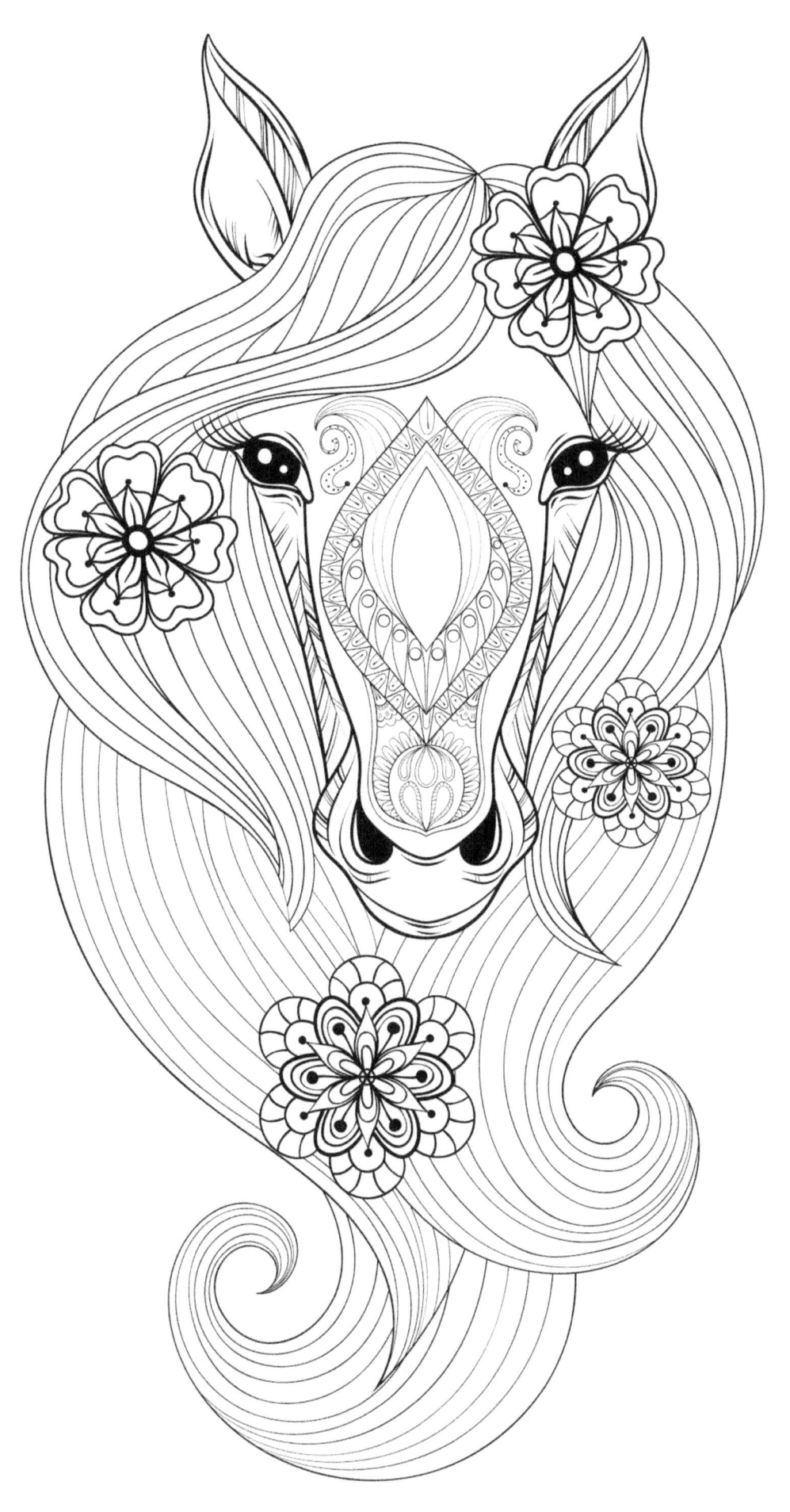

Julia

I gave a little twirl as I crossed the glossy hardwood floor of the living room. I was excited about my date.

"Come see me, my beautiful pearl." My dad looked tired from his shift as on-call doctor at the hospital. He stood, tall for someone of Japanese descent, slender as a reed, and opened his arms. I laid my head against his chest, breathing in the smell of antiseptic that clung to him even after he'd changed his clothes.

My mother smiled at us as she glided past and in that moment, happy and safe in my protective clamshell, I couldn't imagine a life any different.

I didn't know, then, that shells could crack.

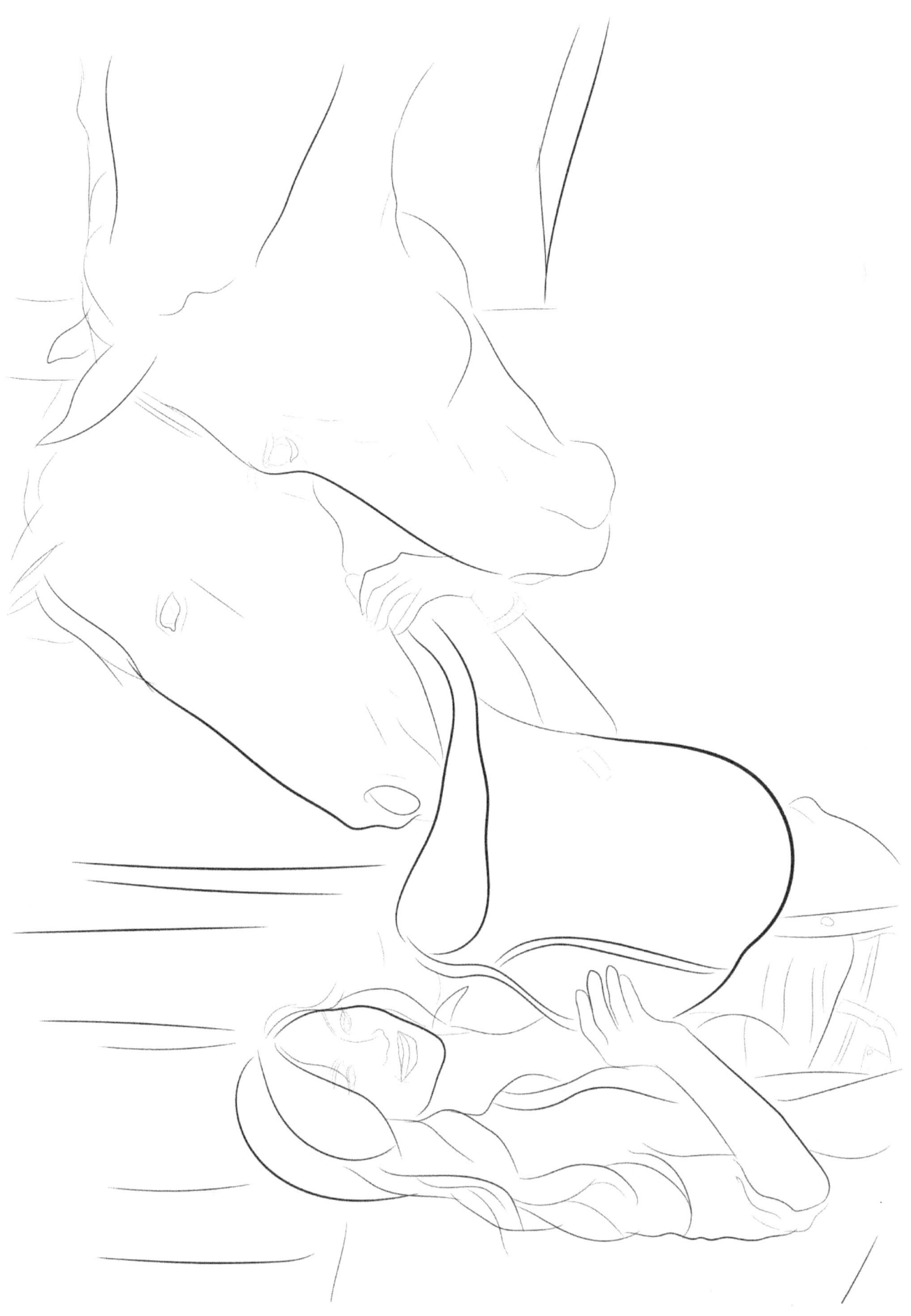

The only emotions that belong in the saddle are patience and a sense of humor.

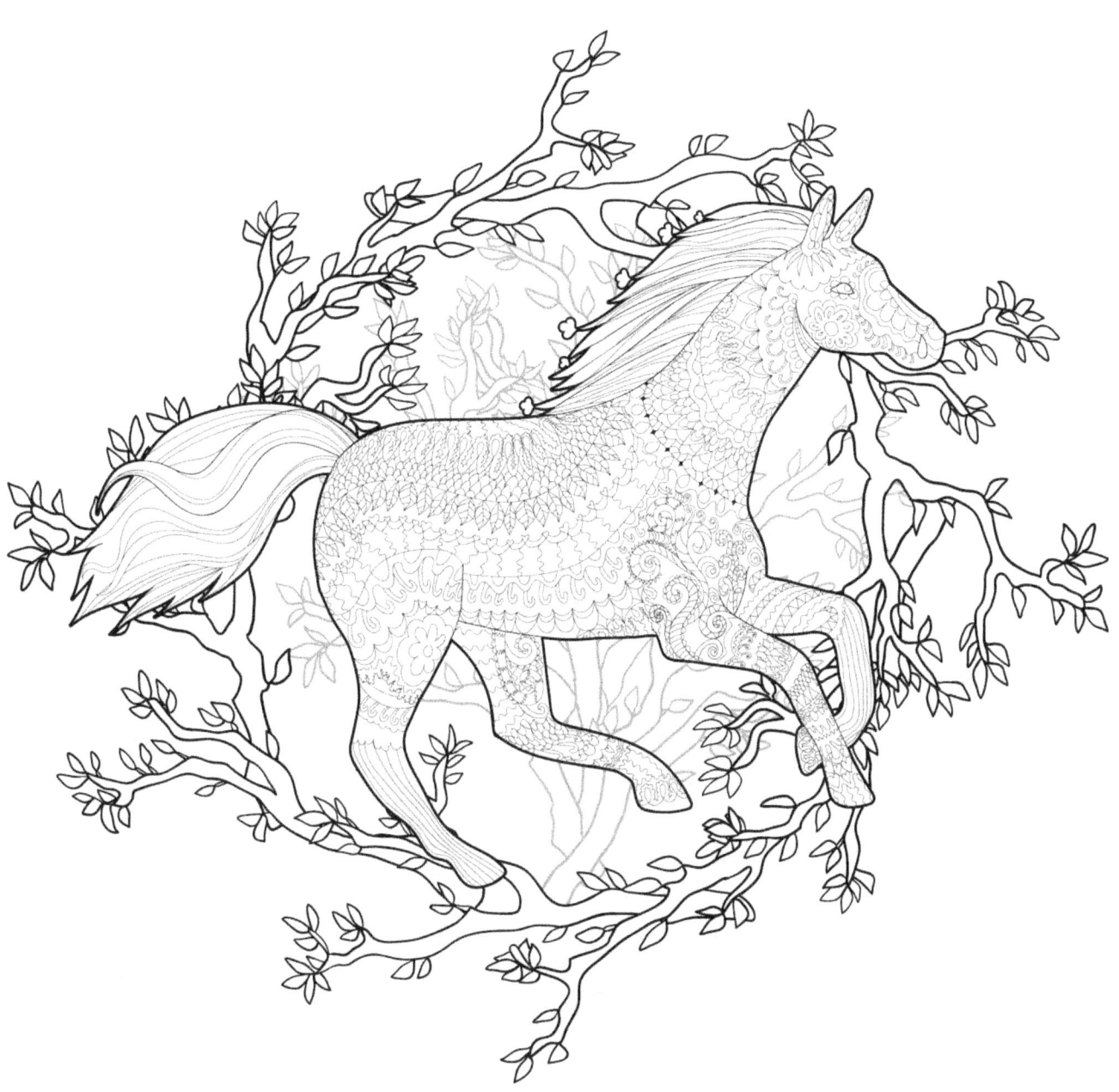

What a wonderful world it would be if people had hearts like dogs.

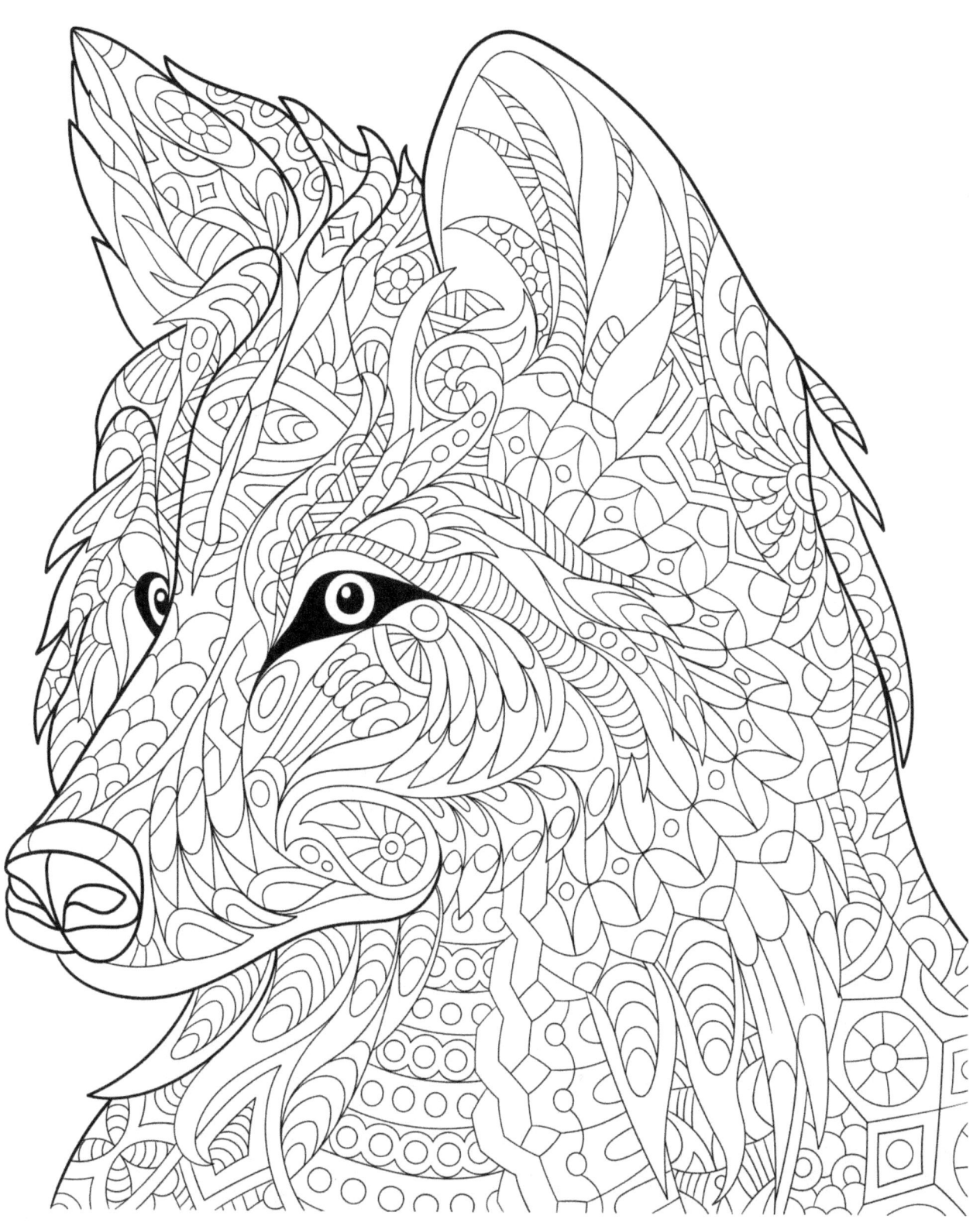

Song of the Horse

How joyous his neigh!
Lo, the Turquoise Horse of Johano-ai,
How joyous his neigh,
There on precious hides outspread standeth he;
How joyous his neigh,
There on tips of fair fresh flowers feedeth he;
How joyous his neigh,
There of mingled waters holy drinketh he;
How joyous his neigh,
There he spurneth dust of glittering grains;
How joyous his neigh,
There in mist of sacred pollen hidden, all hidden he;
How joyous his neigh,
There his offspring many grow and thrive for evermore;
How joyous his neigh!

– Navajo Song

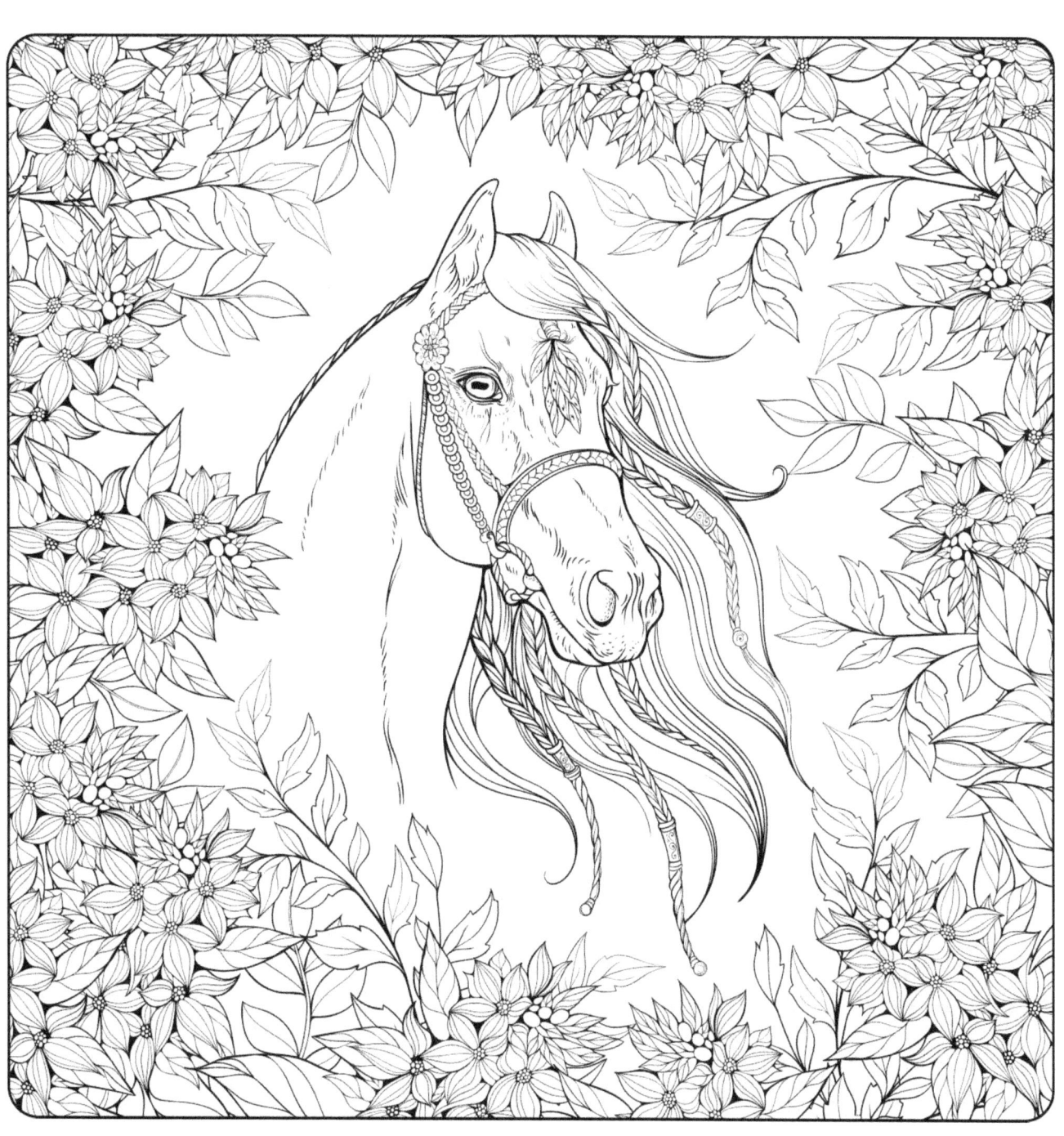

Jaden

Jaden would probably be voted "sexiest man alive" if he were an actor. The thing is, he'd never act. He truly *lives* more than anyone I know. Whether he's doing a breathless, heart-hammering gallop down the polo field or singing in the kitchen as he cooks, he's fully "there."

Physical beauty always fades, but the bright luster of true beauty never dulls. No matter his age, Jaden's effulgence will be dazzling.

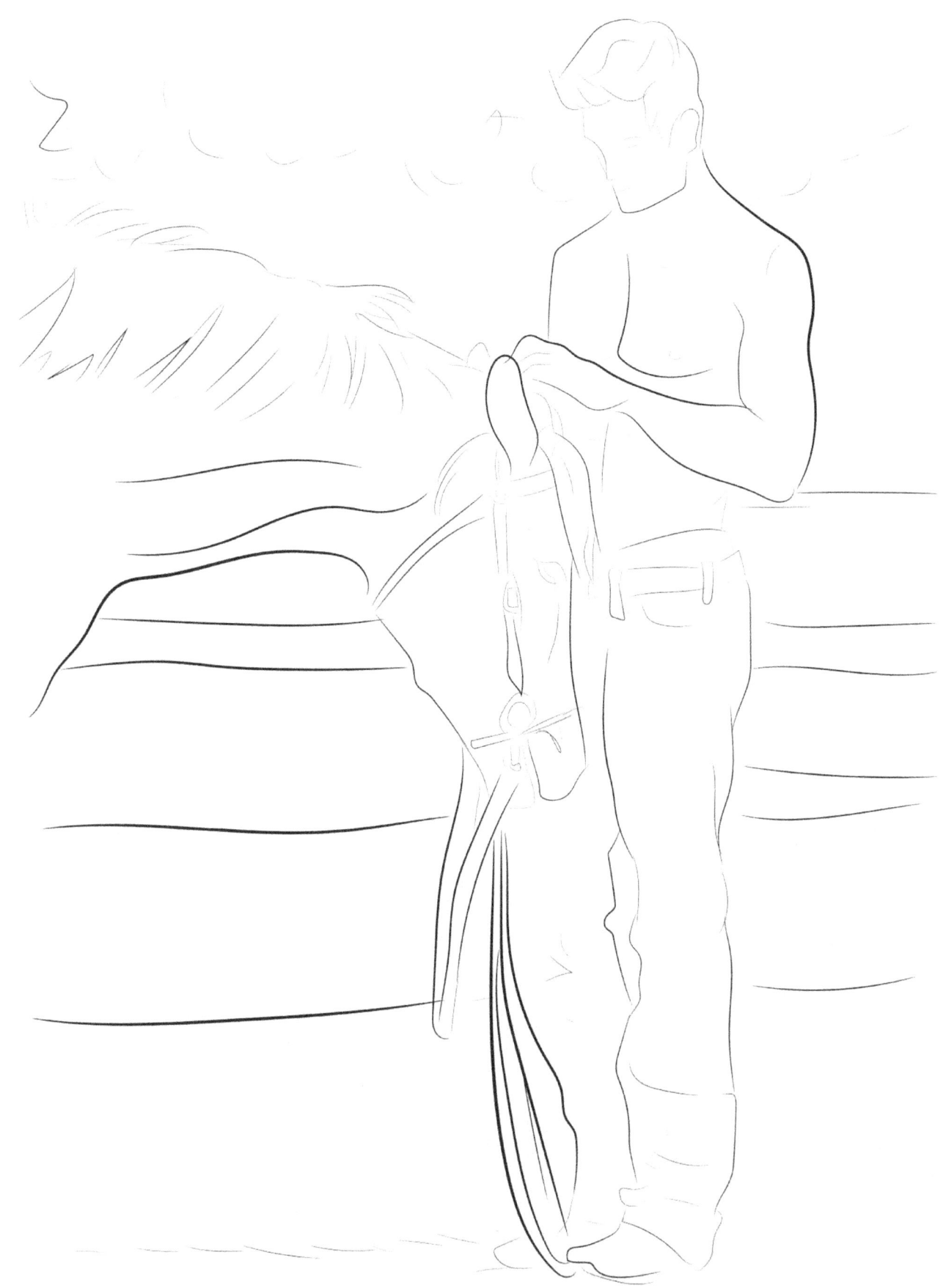

"Crazy Horse dreamed and went into the world where there is nothing but the spirits of all things. That is the real world that is behind this one, and everything we see here is something like a shadow from that one." – Black Elk

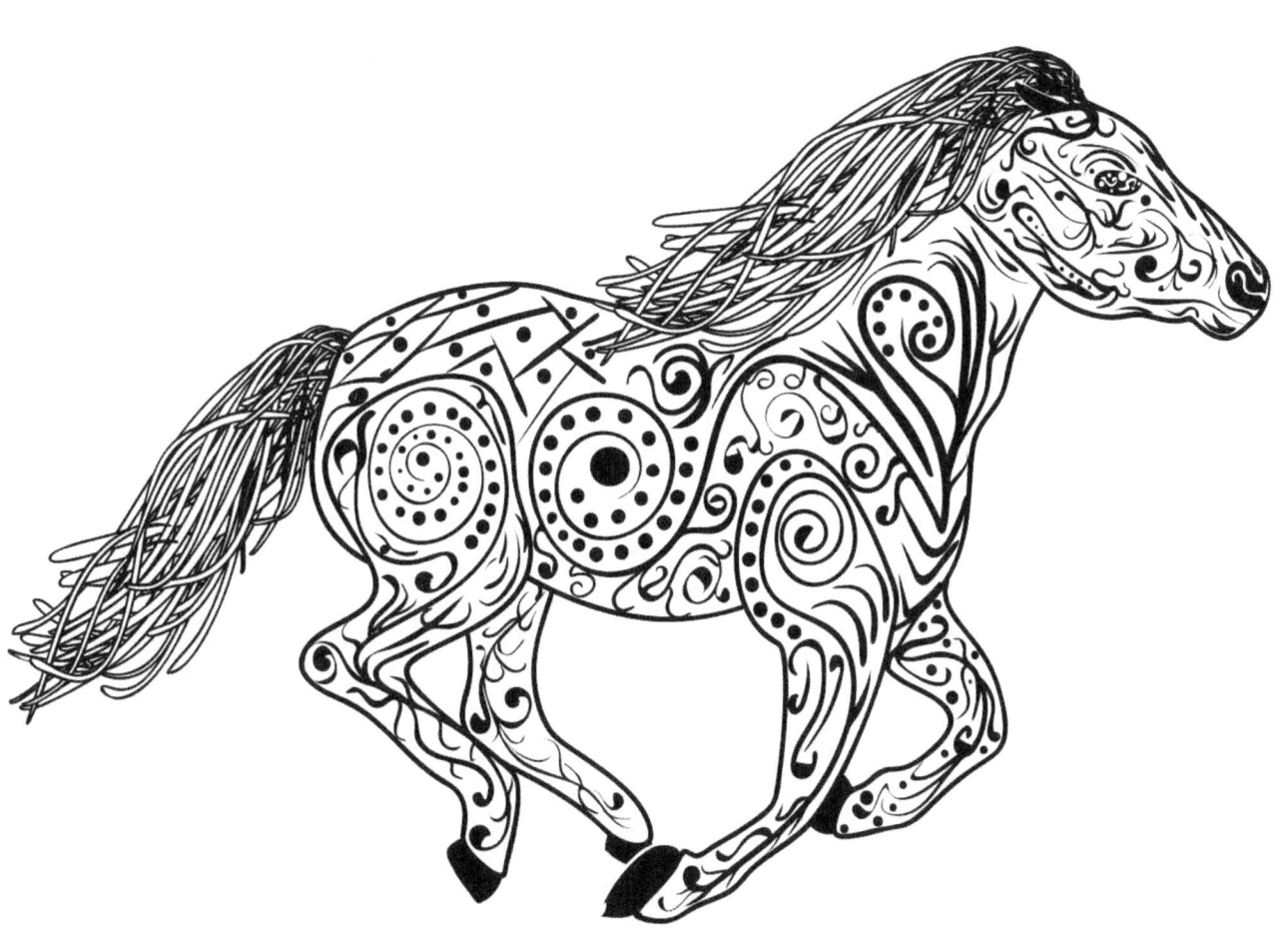

"If you have good thoughts they will shine out of your face like sunbeams and you will always look lovely." – Roald Dahl

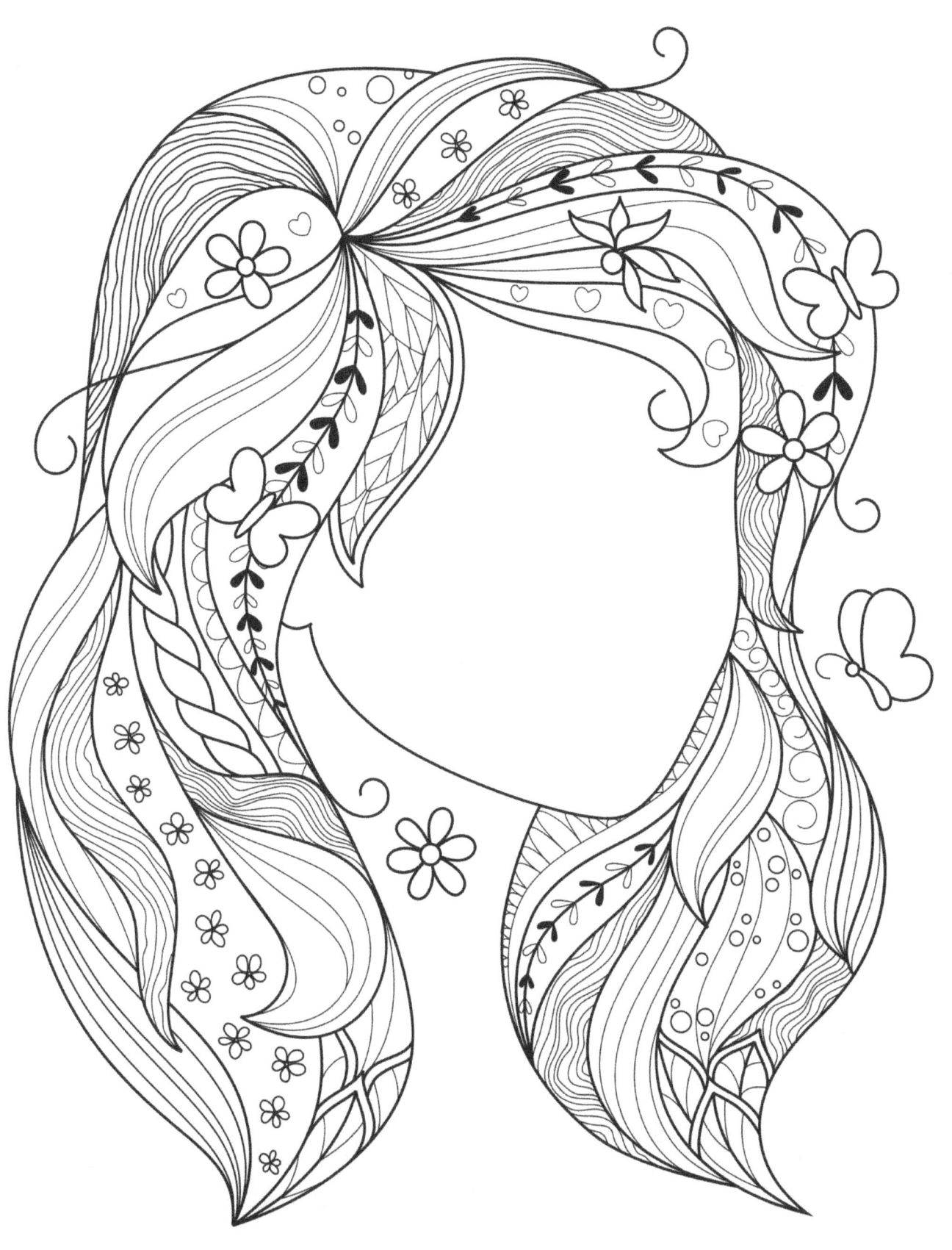

Teri

Some people are quiet heros. They walk around strewing the world with good deeds. They're kind without expectations, helpful without being asked, they listen without judgment.

Or, they can be the kind of friend who makes you laugh until juice squirts out your nose. And then takes a picture.

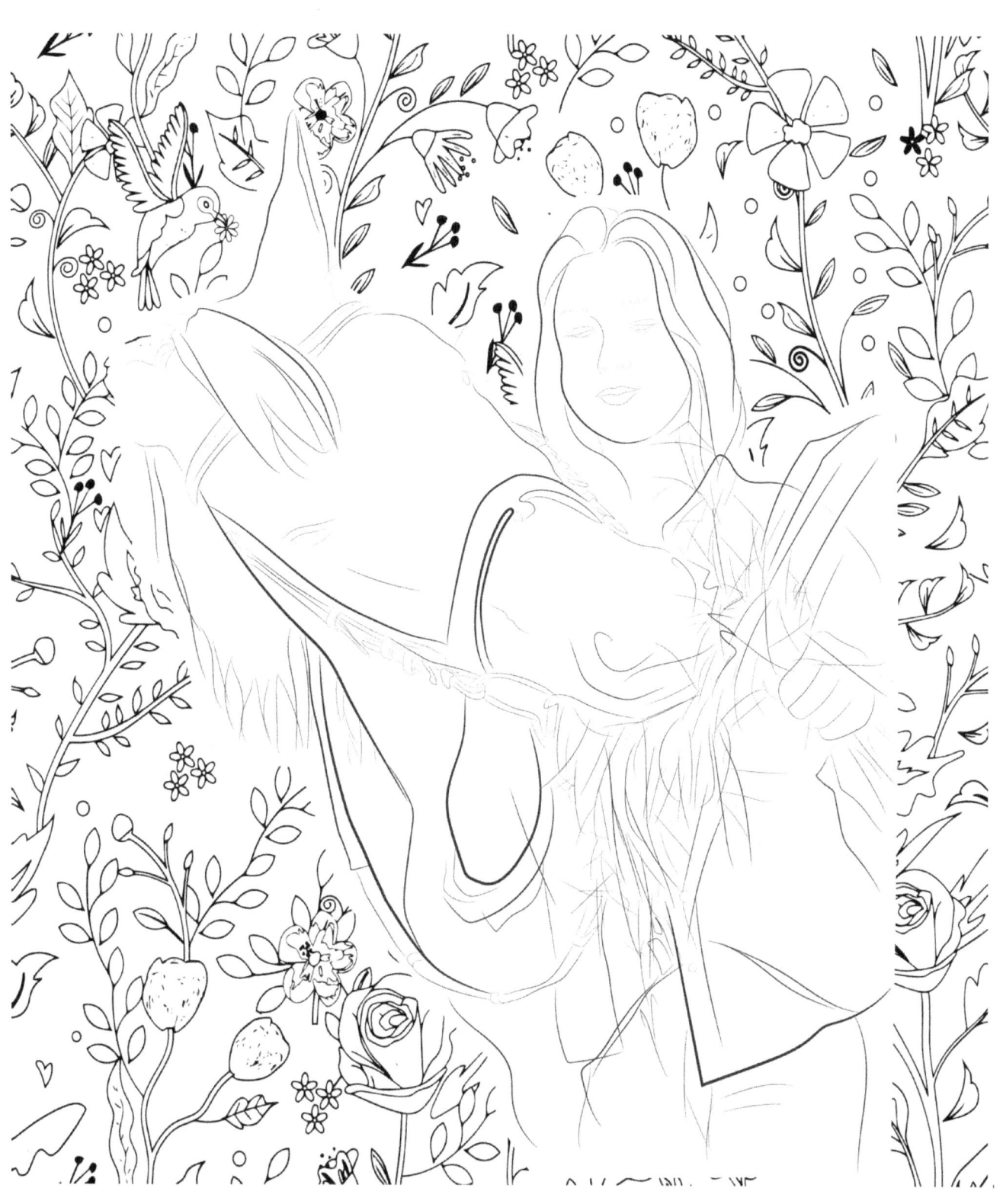

Dec and Elina

The time they had together was short, when compared to a lifetime. But love fills our sails and sets us off in new directions. It's never to be regretted.

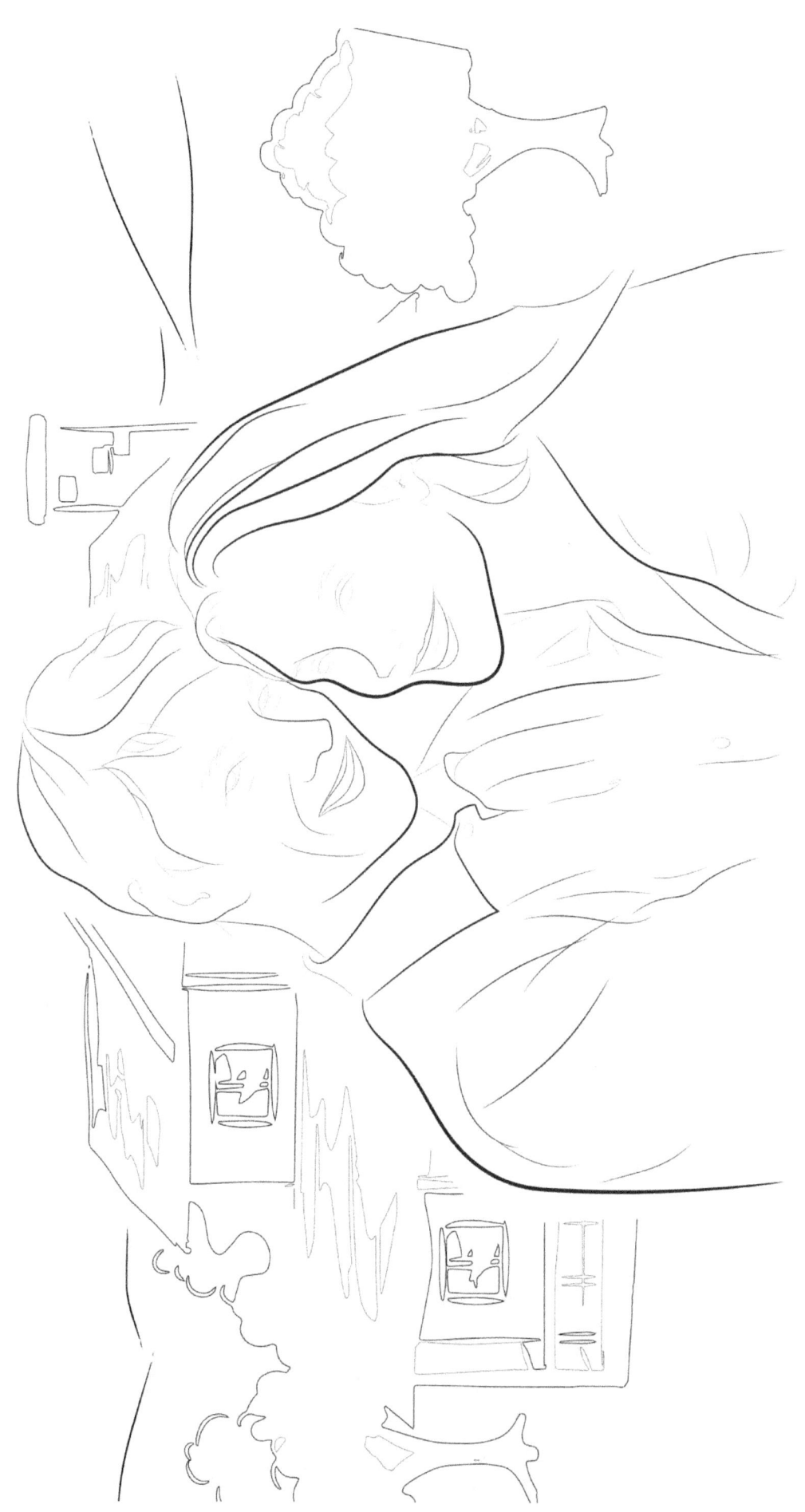

The magic of horses is something that can't be explained to those who don't feel it. It's an emotion that can't be spoken, and the very act of trying to describe it somehow diminishes it.

Some people are horse-magic muggles, and that's okay. Horses deserve to be adored by those who truly appreciate them.

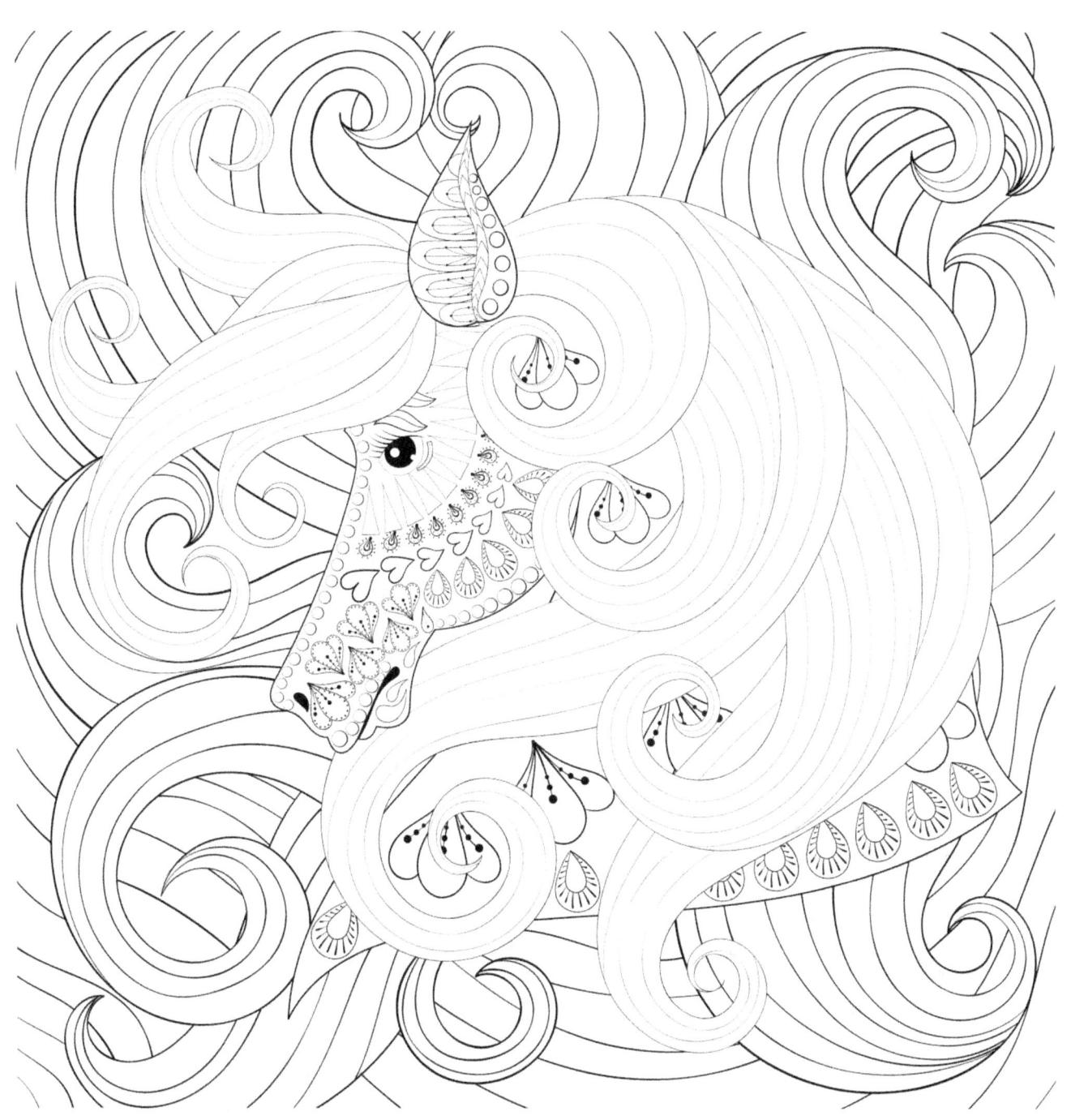

The characters in this coloring book are from the book series *Blaze of Glory* by M. Garzon.

When she's not hiking up the sides of active volcanos in the company of stray dogs, M. Garzon likes to take time to appreciate the fierce beauty of the natural world around her. A rebel at heart, she's not above enjoying the simple pleasures in life, such as telling a good story or sneaking chocolate into the movie theater. She shares her home with two kids and five rescue animals.

Website: www.mgarzon.ca

Facebook: @MGarzonAuthor

Books by M. Garzon:

Blaze of Glory

Look Twice

Renaissance Man

Elina

Halo Boy

For kids 8-12:

Awesome Possum

Lemon Squeezy

www.ingramcontent.com/pod-product-compliance
Lightning Source LLC
Chambersburg PA
CBHW062235220526
45471CB00009B/3486